ARCHANGELOLOGY
VIOLET FLAME
ONENESS

IF YOU CALL THEM THEY WILL COME

KIM CALDWELL

Archangelology LLC

A Division of Archangelology LLC

https://archangelology.com

Introduction Editing and enhancement Rachel Caldwell

Book Editing Grammarly

ISBN: 978-1-947284-22-7

Book Cover Picture Nicola Zalewski

Cover Design Kim Caldwell

Created with Vellum

ABOUT THE SERIES

"Logic will get you from point A to B. Imagination will take you everywhere."-- Einstein

This piece is one of a series of Angelic Upgrade books that fill you with Divine Angelic codes. Angelic laws are based on love and light thus, operate for free-will, so we must call and ask the Archangels for help.

When working with your book relax, take deep breaths and ground to Mother Earth. Focus on Intentions for whatever it is your heart desires that are for the highest good of all involved. Intentions for these energies that we can not see but feel when we are ready. There are those that believe The Archangels are the Ones that make Law of Attraction Work.

This series of books take on a life of its own as the Archangels move and play from book to book, creating a Delicious Alchemy. Each book becomes an instrument in this Celestial Symphony for a more fulfilling life. Many of the Archangel books also carry and infuse the Violet Flame and Divine Connection to Mother Earth for a transformational experience.

Each book has a matching meditation audio available for your listening pleasure at https://archangelology.com/home Please visit our site for your gifts. The book and the audio have similar wording, yet according to the Archangels, they Upgrade us differently. Each medium has a unique experience, energetically Upgrading us in distinct ways. Each time you read or hear an Archangel Upgrade, a new dimension is added or adjusted for your benefit.

Become interactive with your book; when inspired, read the words aloud, and let them roll over you, feeling the love and magic that the Angels radiate. When inspired create your own rituals; there is no right or wrong way. As you play with the rock stars of the Celestial realm, you can expect your life to become more heavenly, more peaceful.

You may Notice Many Words are Uniquely Capitalized throughout this series; this is yet another way the Angels infuse us. When you see this try to feel that word or phrase; sensing the depth of its Intensity of Pure Divine Light throughout your Being.

The Archangel Energy is neither male nor female. This gender fluidity is made clear in this series by the use of the word they or she/he to convey a non-gender energy that shifts roles to uplift and nurture you. The upgrades happen in Divine Time, and there is no schedule. There is no competition. There is no rush. Wherever you are in the process is perfect.

A word about the length of this book. "Less is more." This Series of books is the result of decades of study in the art of Law of

Attraction, Angelic knowing and energy healing, condensed here for you in a format that will shift and benefit the reader. If you found your way here, you can expect miracles. As Einstein said, "There are only two ways to live your life. One is as though nothing is a miracle. The other is as though everything is a miracle." The matching audio to this book is 44 minutes, so working with that is always an option.

Both Neville Goddard and Albert Einstein stated that our imagination is the creative force. Goddard went so far as to imply that our imagination is the God/dess Energy. I mention this to you because as you read these words with much more than your eyes, let your imagination run wild with vivid pictures of the love the magical Archangels have for you and of your adventures together. Enjoy.

ABOUT THE VIOLET FLAME

Elizabeth Clare Prophet said, if we invoke the Violet Flame in our lives on a daily basis, in a period of six months, we will not recognize our life because it will become so wonderful and blessed. All the Archangels join this exciting journey to help us heal with the Violet Flame. We take this opportunity to set boundaries and let certain individuals or things leave our lives; this is okay now. Take deep healing breaths as you allow the Violet Flame to come in and clear and heal your life with the Archangels assistance and Divine guidance. We wish everyone nothing but health, peace, bliss, love, and light because as we desire this for others, the same radiates back to us. Zadkiel, the keeper of the Violet Flame, makes a special guest appearance and brings their Violet Flame Dragons to help clear anything that no longer serves us. St Germain, the keeper of the Violet Flame, joins us as well for masterful teachings. All the Archangels work with the Violet Flame to create Oneness and vibrate a signal for more love, peace, and abundance. We partner with this Divine Wisdom with the assistance of these enlightened beings for amazing results over time. Adapting these mindsets will help shift your consciousness and make you a magnet for confidence, peace, and prosperity in new refreshed ways. There is no right or wrong way to use this tool. All these Divinely Intelligent Angelic Upgrades happen with grace and ease at the individual's comfortable pace. The only thing I recommend you keep in the forefront of your practice is to ensure you are enjoying the process. Meet the Archangels in the Archangelology Book and Audio Series that is here to help you at this time. If you call on the Violet Flame, it will come, just as all of the Divine energy will come to your assistance when beckoned. Spending time with Archangels creates a heavenly life. For gifts from the Archangels visit https://archangelology.com/home

VIOLET FLAME ONENESS

Archangelology, Violet Flame. It is said by Elizabeth Clare Prophet that if we invoke the Violet Flame in our lives on a daily basis, over a period of six months, we won't be able to recognize our life anymore because it will become so wonderful and blessed. It is also known in the ancient, ancient teachings, that if we call the Archangels, the Enlightened Masters, the Benevolent Beings, they will come. There is a Divine Process by which you can call your Archangels, Ascended Masters, or any Divine Beings you choose, and they will hear you even better. As you call their names, you will see lightning coming to you and igniting you, sending you a magical light, a brilliant energy. So as you say the name, for instance, Archangel Gabriel, right as you say Gabriel, you will see lightning igniting you. You will know your Angel can see, hear, and feel you, and he will come right as you call. This will create more Angelic Magic in your life.

Today, let us rise above any fear matrix, any illusion, and spend some time with the Angels in the Violet Flame. Let us do this for the highest good of all involved, for the best, and with strong intentions to plant the seeds that will create a better life. Let us start by grounding and sealing ourselves in light. First, see roots going deep into the ground. Ground yourself and take a deep, healing breath. Now, we will invoke Angels as we do this on a daily basis, our lives will become magical and blessed. On your left, please ask Archangel Michael to stand beside you. See Michael in all of his/her glory. See Michael with his/her left arm over his/her chest, holding a light sword. See the sword; it is so

bright, so sparkly, so beautiful, and so powerful. Ignite it. Now, see Michael holding
his/her other arm straight in front of him/her,
with his/her sword pointing out and
protecting you. Michael may appear to you as
a female or a male. Pick the one that makes
you feel the safest and the most powerful.
Take a deep, healing breath.

Now, on your right, see Archangel Raziel.
Call Archangel Raziel. Archangel Raziel is
the Archangel of Knowledge and Wisdom.
See Archangel Raziel standing on your right
side, protecting and surrounding your aura.
Take a deep, healing breath. Now, please see
a beautiful light starting in your chest, at
your heart chakra. Watch it glow a beautiful
Violet Flame color. Now, watch as this Violet
Flame glows and becomes bigger and bigger,
and surrounds you and your beautiful
Angels, a cool, soothing Violet fire, Violet
Flame, all around you, and creating a beautiful globe, protecting, healing, sealing,
creating a safe boundary between you and
anything negative or unwanted. Take a deep,
healing breath.

Practice this daily. You may work with any

Archangels you would like to stand beside you, any Angels you need. In the Archangelology Series, there are many Archangels here for you, ready to work with you, to lift you, to bring you into wholeness, to bring you into oneness, to bring you back into the powerful magical creator that you are. Take a deep, healing breath. Now, together we will spend some time invoking the Violet Flame. You may say this with me aloud, or you may say this to yourself. You may find other ways to say it. Be creative with it, and visualize as we say this. See the Violet Flame all around you. See the Violet Flame throughout your environment. See the Violet Flame throughout your home. See the Violet Flame throughout your work, throughout your play, throughout your family. See it throughout any situations that have challenged you; let the Violet Flame go in and do its magical, transformative, transmuting work so that miracles can happen.

Say with me now, to yourself or out loud. "I am the Violet Flame in action. I am the Violet Flame. I am the Violet Flame in action. I am the Violet Flame. I am the light of God's creation. I am the Violet Flame. I am the light of Goddess creation. I am the Violet Flame. I am, I am, I am, I am, I am the Violet Flame. I am, I am, I am, I am, I am the Violet Flame. I am, I am, I am I am, I am the Violet Flame. I am, I am, I am, I am, I am the Violet Flame. I am the light of God's creation. I am the Violet Flame. I am the light of Goddess' creation. I am the Violet Flame. I am, I am, I am, I am, I am the Violet Flame."

Now as we speak this, see the Violet Fire all around you. See the Violet Flame engulfing your life. See your hands filled with Violet Flame. See your body shimmering with beautiful Violet Flame. "I am the light of God's creation. I am the Violet Flame. I am the light of Goddess' creation. I am the Violet Flame. I am I am I am I am I am the Violet Flame. I am I am I am I am I am the Violet Flame. I am I am I am I am I am the Violet Flame. I am I am I am I am I am the Violet Flame. I am the light of God's creation. I am the Violet Flame. I am the light of Goddess creation. I am the Violet Flame. I am I am I am I am I am the Violet Flame. I am I am I am I am I am the Violet

Flame. I am I am I am I am I am the Violet Flame."

Now, see Archangel Raphael standing beside you on your left side. Take a deep, healing breath. Archangel Raphael is the Archangel of health and abundance. We're going to now actively bring health and abundance into our lives as we wish. Blessings happen as we infuse our world and the Universe with the gorgeous Violet Flame. Say it with me now: "I am the Violet Flame in action. I am the Violet Flame. I am the light of God's creation. I am the Violet Flame. I am the light of Goddess' creation. I am the Violet Flame. I am, I am, I am, I am, I am the Violet Flame. I am, I am, I am, I am, I am the Violet Flame. I am, I am, I am, I am, I am the Violet Flame. I am the light of God's creation. I am the Violet Flame. I am, I am, I am, I am, I am the Violet Flame. I am the light of God's creation. I am the Violet Flame. I am the light of Goddess' creation. I am the Violet Flame. I am, I am, I am, I am, I am the Violet Flame."

Now, take a deep healing breath. Now, let us invoke the gorgeous Archangel Metatron. Please ask Archangel Metatron, who is the

Archangel of so many things, "Archangel Metatron, help us, heal us with sacred geometry." Archangel Metatron helps heal children, helps heal lives. Please call on Archangel Metatron as we do this Violet Flame together. See Archangel Metatron standing beside you, and see the Violet Flame engulfing you. As you do this, set the deep intention for more peace, more love light in your lives.

Here we go." I am the Violet Flame in action. I am the Violet Flame. I am the light of God's creation. I am the Violet Flame. I am I am I am I am I am the Violet Flame. I am I am I am I am the Violet Flame. I am I am I am I am I am the Violet Flame. I am I am I am I am I am the Violet Flame. I am the light of Goddess creation. I am the Violet Flame. I am the Violet Flame. I am the light of Goddess creation. I am the Violet Flame. I am the light of God's creation. I am the Violet Flame. I am the light of God's creation. I am the Violet Flame. I am I am I am I am I am the Violet Flame."

Now, take a deep, healing breath. When inspired, lift your hand, and feel the Violet

Flames moving through you. Feel your deep connection to the Source, remembering that no person, place, or thing is the Source of our supply of Divine energy. The God or Goddess energy is the Source or our supply. Take a deep, healing breath. Now, let us call Archangel Camael. Archangel Camael is the Archangel of courage. Whenever we need courage in our lives, let us call Archangel Camael to help us invoke this quality in us, so that we be brave, show courage, and make wise, brilliant decisions that enhance our lives and those of the people around us. Let us do this while we invoke the Violet Flame, asking Archangel Camael to help us now. Take a deep healing breath. Hold up your hand and invoke the Divine Violet Flame with me now.

"I am the Violet Flame in action. I am the Violet Flame. I am the Violet Flame in action. I am the Violet Flame. I am the Violet Flame in action. I am the Violet Flame. I am the light of God's creation. I am the Violet Flame. I am the light of God's creation. I am the Violet Flame. I am I am I am I am I am the Violet Flame. I am I am I am I am I am the Violet Flame. I am I am I am I am I am the Violet Flame. I am the light of God's creation. I am the Violet Flame. I am the light of God's creation. I am the Violet Flame. I am, I am, I am, I am, I am the Violet Flame."

Now, see this Violet Fire brilliantly burning all around you, transmuting any negative energies, transmuting anything that no longer serves you. See it and ask Camael to stand by your side. Take a deep healing breath. Feel that Violet Flame. I want you to call to mind now anyone or any situation in your life where you felt bullied. Pull it into your mind now, see it. Take a deep healing breath. You are safe. Camael is by your side. We are going to invoke the Divine Power of the Violet Flame to clear and heal any bullies, any bullying from your life. Take a deep healing breath. See Camael standing beside you. See how magnificent he/she in her/his power. See Camael standing there, strong, by your side. See your heart chakra emanating a beautiful, beautiful red light, like Camael's. Watch it fill you completely, the red light, and then go out and create a bubble around you.

Take a deep breath. See that person, or situation where you feel bullied, see it now in front of you. See them standing very still and looking at you. Then, all of a sudden, Archangel Camael screams your name as loud as she/he can right in his or her ear. Now, see that person confused? He or she doesn't know what to do. Take a deep breath. See yourself calm, poised. See Archangel Camael's hand on your shoulder, protecting you. Hold that image. Hold that image.

Now, see that other person walking away from you, and feel the relief. See Archangel Michael standing on your other side. See Archangel Michael placing a bubble of light around you and one around that person and see Archangel Michael cutting all strings between you and that person or situation, letting it go, letting it leave your life. Take a deep breath. Very good. Now, once again, let us invoke the Violet Flame together.

"I am the Violet Flame in action. I am the Violet Flame." See the Violet Flame engulfing the situation. See everything being filled with Violet fire, cleansing and healing, yes, transmuting, changing to something higher. See that person either shifting or changing or leaving your life. See them gone for now. "I am the Violet Flame in action. I am the Violet Flame." See the situation gone for now. "I am the Violet Flame in action. I am the Violet Flame. I am the light of God's creation. I am the light of Goddess creation. I am the Violet Flame. I am, I am, I am, I am, I am the Violet Flame. I am, I am, I am, I am, I am the Violet Flame. I am, I am, I am, I am, I am the Violet Flame. Feel it. I am, I am, I am, I am, I am the Violet Flame." Feel your power. "I am, I am, I am, I am, I am the Violet Flame. I am the light of God/Goddess creation. I am the Violet Flame." Yes, feel it. Know it is done. Relax.

Now, take some deep healing breaths. Relax. You're safe now. Feel your power. You have Archangels as your friends and the beautiful Saint Germain, Keeper of the Violet Flame, as a friend. We only wish good for everyone. We want the best for all involved. But if it is time to set boundaries and let certain people leave our lives, this is okay now. Take deep healing breaths. Allow the

Violet Flame to come in, and the Archangels, to do this with ease, with grace, with joy, with peace, with bliss, with Divine guidance. We wish everyone nothing but health, peace, bliss, love, and light because as we wish this for others, the same comes back to us.

However, we also understand that we can put firmly in place boundaries, guards, wards, and we invoke and activate this knowing now. We use this Divine wisdom. King Solomon, one of the most resourceful, majestic kings in history, spent much time invoking Divine beings and angels. He spent a lot of time with Archangel Haniel. Archangel Haniel is the angel of magic and love. Take a deep healing breath. When we call Archangel Haniel into our lives, we can expect more love, juicier, delicious relationships, and more self-love. We can give ourselves a break. We can love ourselves more. We can invoke this now. We can ask Archangel Haniel to shift our self-talk, to help us talk lovingly to ourselves, to help us hear when we're not talking lovingly to ourselves. Archangel Haniel, we ask that you come and do this for us now. And we ask that you help us invoke the Violet Flame to transmute any crevices, any small areas in us that have not learned to love deeply and sweetly. See Archangel Haniel in all the glory standing to your left side.

With me now, invoke the beautiful Violet Flame. Take a deep breath. Hold the intention of deep, sweet love in your life and say, "I am the Violet Flame in action; I am the Violet Flame. I am the light of God's creation. I am the Violet Flame. I am, I am, I am, I am, I am the Violet Flame. I am the Violet Flame in action; I am the Violet Flame. I am the light of God's creation. I am the Violet Flame. I am, I am, I am, I am, I am the Violet Flame. I am the light of God's creation. I am the Violet Flame. I am, I am, I am, I am, I am the Violet Flame. I am the light of God's creation. I am the Violet Flame. I am, I am, I am, I am, I am the Violet Flame. I am, I am, I am, I am, I am the Violet Flame."

Take a deep healing breath. Feel it. See the Violet Flame all around you. See the Violet Flame transmuting any areas of your heart, of your mind, of your body, of your spirit, to love yourself more. See your magnificence. See your brilliance and allow yourself to share it with others. Deep, healing breath. Yes, beautiful, beautiful work. Divine Work.

Now, I would like to call in the beautiful Archangel Jophiel. Archangel Jophiel, in the Archangelology series, works with us on not judging ourselves and not judging others. And we're going to call her/him in now, and we're going to invoke some Violet Flame, and we're going to ask for help. We're going to invoke the knowing, and we're going to use it often. "I now allow the Goddess/God in me to release all judgments of myself and anyone else." Feel that, anchor it, and use that invocation when you find yourself judging yourself or others. Also, we're going to call on a team of fairies.

Archangel Jophiel, please bring in a team of benevolent, loving, white-light, beautiful fairies that will work with us. And at any time we find ourselves judging ourselves harshly or judging others harshly, we would like to bring in and invoke the Violet Flame and say this beautiful, healing phrase and see all judgment, all harsh feelings, gently transmuting with ease, with peace. Feel your mind, body, and spirit. Now, take a deep breath. Say it with me now, and see that Violet Flame burning away any judgment, any prejudice, any racism that no longer serves us. See the Violet Flame release any ageism, any gender bias, any inequality. See the Violet Flame now. Let's do it together with Archangel Jophiel and our team of beautiful, benevolent fairies. Take a deep breath.

"I am the Violet Flame in action; I am the Violet Flame. I am, I am, I am, I am, I am the Violet Flame. I am, I am, I am, I am, I am the Violet Flame." Feel the Violet Flame tickling your body. "I am, I am, I am, I am, I am the Violet Flame. Yes, I am, I am, I am, I am, I am the Violet Flame. I am the light of God's creation. I am the Violet Flame. I am the light of Goddess creation. I am the Violet Flame. I am, I am, I am, I am, I am the Violet Flame. I am, I am, I am, I am, I am the Violet Flame. Feel it. I am, I am, I am, I am, I am the Violet Flame. I am, I am, I am, I am, I am the Violet Flame." Yes. Feel it. Infuse yourself with it.

Deep, healing breath. Beautiful. Now, we're working the Violet Flame all throughout our minds, our bodies, our spirits. We're working the Violet Flame all throughout our lives. As we invoke the Violet Flame, we understand that this is a call for peace in our lives, for happiness in our lives, for blessings for us and everyone around us. And we're also calling this for our world. As we invoke the Violet Flame, we are clearing the fear matrix, healing others, connecting with others like us, connecting with like minds, creating beautiful healing.

And we're going to call in the gorgeous, Divine Archangel Uriel to help us. Archangel Uriel is the Princess/Prince of peace. We can take Archangel Uriel with us to any room, to any place, to any city. We can call and invoke Archangel Uriel and bring great peace to that area, to our lives, and to the lives of people that we love. Archangel Uriel is also a master at protecting us. When we need to feel safe, we can call Archangel Uriel, and we can see her/him standing at our left side. We can see her/his Divine light-sword crossed over her/his chest. We can see her/his protection surrounding us and filling us with peace. Take a deep healing breath.

Now we ask that Archangel Uriel works with us and helps us to invoke this Violet Flame. We do the invocation now together. Deep healing breath. Set the intention for peace in your life and Universal peace. Deep healing breath. Say it with me now: "I am the Violet Flame in action. I am the Violet Flame. I am the light of God's creation. I am the Violet Flame. I am I am I am I am I am the Violet Flame. I am I am I am I am I am the Violet Flame. I am I am I am I am I am the Violet Flame." See that Violet Flame running through your life, running through your world, running through the Universe now. Yes. Deep healing breath.

"I am the Violet Flame in action. I am the Violet Flame. I am the Violet Flame in action. I am the Violet Flame. I am the light of God's creation. I am the Violet Flame. I am the light of God's creation. I am the Violet Flame. I am I am I am I am I am the Violet Flame. I am, I am, I am, I am, I am the Violet Flame." Yes. Take a deep breath. Now plant that seed, that intention, for peace, for joy, for bliss, for Divine abundance in your life and the life of your loved ones. Now, hold that intention. Water that intention with Violet Fire and light so that it may grow. So that you may shine and be the Divine Being that the Angels already know you are. So that confidence can seep out of you into the world and fill your heart and fill your mind and fill your body. Take a deep healing breath.

Now we're going to do a Divine Action that if you choose to do daily, you will feel much better in all aspects of your mind, body, and spirit. We're going to balance our chakras with Divine Light, and we're going to do this with the assistance of Archangel Zadkiel. Zadkiel is an amazing Archangel. He is the Angel of the Violet Flame. And Archangel Zadkiel has Violet Flame dragons. So we ask that Archangel Zadkiel stand beside us now to our right, and we ask that Archangel Zadkiel face us as we face her/him. And we see our chakra system, and we're going to have Archangel Zadkiel light it up and heal it now. But Zadkiel wants us to know something. Zadkiel wants us to know that this is something we can do ourselves. This is our chakra system. This is our balancing system, and we can bring it into

Divine Balance anytime we choose. And as we practice doing this, it will become easier and easier.

First, watch as Archangel Zadkiel helps you ground yourself. Shoot your grounding cord deep into the Earth. See roots going into the ground. Archangel Zadkiel is standing before you and pointing to your base chakra. That is the chakra right at the base of your spine. Take a deep healing breath. Yes. Archangel Zadkiel is helping you spin your energy there in a beautiful red swirl. Spinning it, balancing it. Perfect. See that area of your body now. We want to infuse it. Watch as Archangel Zadkiel infuses it with Confidence, with a ruby, with roses, yes. Deep healing breath. And feel its balance.

Now, move right up to the chakra in between your belly button and that area Archangel Zadkiel is pointing at. It is a glowing, beautiful orange color. See it glowing. See it spinning. See it balancing. And watch as Archangel Zadkiel sends sunshine and citrine to that area. Yes, feel it balance. Now let's move up to your belly button, and watch as Archangel Zadkiel is pointing to that area.

She/He is filling that area with Divine Yellow Light. And you watch as it circles and balances, and you feel your confidence rise. Yes. Watch as citrine and more sunshine are channeled to that area, and you feel so relaxed, so good, so confident.

Now watch as Archangel Zadkiel's hand moves up to your heart chakra. Yes. This area is spinning, balanced, green. Watch as Archangel Zadkiel fills that area with the Divine Light of emeralds. Feel your heart opening. Zadkiel now reminds you that you will use this area as your thinking mechanism. You will think with your heart chakra, thus creating a loving, balanced life. Take a deep healing breath. Now watch as Archangel Zadkiel moves her/his Divine Fingers to your throat chakra. She/He balances and swirls the energy. You see blue. It looks beautiful. Archangel Zadkiel sends confidence to speak your truth and say Sweet words to this area, and the wisdom to know the right times to do it. Deep healing breath.

Now, Archangel Zadkiel moves her/his beautiful hand to your third eye, and Violet light is infused in this area. You see that area spinning. You see it balance. You feel amazing. Yes. Excellent. Violets go to that area, anything that makes you smile and feel tingly to help you to see the unseen, to go beyond the five senses, to where the real knowledge and wisdom is. Archangel Zadkiel is activating your third eye and helping you with grace and ease now. Deep healing breath. Now, on top of your head, you're going to see a beautiful, brilliant pink lotus. It's spinning. Yes. It is pure, pink light, a thousand-petal lotus spinning, enlightening you, bringing you peace, bringing you into your power, reminding you who you are. Yes. Feel it. Deep healing breath.

Now, finally, you see a golden light surrounding you like the Sun, enveloping you in a beautiful healing circle of protection. Yes. Deep healing breath. That is it. It is that simple, and once you practice it, you will be able to do it in seconds. Zadkiel wants to remind you that you can balance your chakras any time. Once you start to do this daily, everything in your life will improve mentally, physically, spiritually. Take a deep, healing breath. Archangel Zadkiel and his

Divine Light Dragons will help us once more to activate the Violet Flame. See the Violet Flame all around you. Let it move throughout your life, and let it heal your life on deep levels. Together, now, we say,

"I am the Violet Flame in action. I am the Violet Flame. Feel it. Feel the vibrations. I am the Violet Flame in action. I am the Violet Flame. I am the light of God's creation. I am the Violet Flame. I am, I am, I am, I am, I am the Violet Flame. I am the light of Goddess' creation I am the Violet Flame. I am the light of Goddess' creation I am the Violet Flame. I am, I am, I am, I am, I am the Violet Flame. I am, I am, I am, I am, I am the Violet Flame. I am the light of Goddess' creation I am the Violet Flame. I am the light of Goddess' creation. I am the Violet Flame. I am I am, I am, I am, I am the Violet Flame."

See all of the Archangels and Saint Germain together in a circle around you. Watch as the roll call happens as these Divine Beings surround you with the love and the light that they have for you. And call them in your mind or aloud. Call Archangel Michael to stand around you in a circle of protection. "Archangel Raphael, please stand around me in a circle of protection. Archangel Metatron, please stand around me in a circle of protection. Archangel Camael, please stand around me in a circle of protection. Archangel Gabriel, please stand around me in a circle of protection. Archangel Haniel, please stand around me in a circle of protection. Archangel Raziel, please stand around me in a circle of protection. Archangel Zadkiel, please stand around me in a circle of protection." See them all, lightning around you. "Archangel Uriel, please stand around me in a circle of protection. Archangel Jophiel, please join, and stand around me in a circle of protection."

Now, take a deep healing breath. You are at the center of the most Divine of Places in the Universe at the moment. You are that loved. You are that valued. And allow the energies of these Divine Angels to Permeate your whole being. And allow at the same time the Violet Fire to fill the circle and burn away anything that no longer serves a master like yourself. a Divine Light Master, the Divine Light Master that you are. Feel the

Violet Flame transmuting these energies, the love and light of the Divine Source filling this circle and healing you on a deep level. Imagine your life filled with more love. Imagine your life filled with more peace. Your life is now filled with more abundance, with more health, with more bliss, with more ecstasy. Yes. Deep healing breath.

The string theory, which can be complicated, is made simple here. The string theory says that we're billions of strings. What this means to us is that sound, thought, and energy can transmute and move through these billions of strings that we are. They can transmute us into higher light beings. Yes. It is that simple. As we activate these Archangels, as we activate the Violet Flame, we move into higher realms. We move into the ecstasy, the bliss, the life where things go the way we want them to go, the life where magic abounds, the life where we rise above fear and we remember who we truly are. And just like people can spread negative feelings, like a disease, we can spread this love, this light, this peace everywhere. We can radiate. We can become a beacon.

We can become—we are—at this moment, that beacon, that light. That is the God/dess Source. And we allow this light to flow out to all those around us. And as we come together, because we are connecting now with all the other beings that are on this journey at the same time, as we come together and fill the world with Violet Light and Violet Flame, we transcend this world. We don't have to stay in fear anymore. We can ascend into the higher realms. We remember who we truly are. Yes. It is that simple. We are here to do the Divine Work, the Divine Healing Work that will transmute our lives into everything we want it to be and that will transform the lives of others around us. Deep, healing breath.

In this circle, on the outer rim of our circle, we see our Violet-Flame dragons. Yes, they're benevolent, loving beings, and they're glowing with Violet Flame all around and flying around and creating bliss and joy everywhere they go. They're Violet-Flame dragons and they bring bliss. I want you to watch as they radiate Violet Flame all around you, and you stand in the circle with a tube of

Violet light around you. And the Violet Flame tickles you and makes you feel amazing. As the whole circle of light radiates together, and together again, we say,

"I am the Violet Flame in action; I am the Violet Flame. I am the light of God's creation. I am the Violet Flame. I am the light of God's creation. I am the Violet Flame. I am, I am, I am, I am, I am the Violet Flame. I am, I am, I am, I am, I am the Violet Flame. I am the light of God's creation. I am the Violet Flame. I am the light of God's creation. I am the Violet Flame. I am, I am, I am, I am, I am the Violet Flame. I am, I am, I am, I am, I am the Violet Flame. I am the light of God's creation. I am the Violet Flame. I am, I am, I am, I am, I am the Violet Flame."

From this moment in time and space, you are Divine. You are light. You are so healed, you are so clear, you are so exactly where the God/dess force feels. It's time for us to radiate out a signal of Oneness. And let me remind you that as you, as I, as we make Oneness our intention in this life, we raise ourselves to higher vibrations. As we let go and stay in Oneness more, our lives become so much more wonderful, so much better. Now, see all your Archangels around you, see Saint Germain, your Violet Angels, and your Violet dragons. And see everything vibrating so fast. See the whole group becoming one. Oneness as the God/dess force shines a light down upon it, upon us, upon our Oneness. Watch as this circle radiates and fills us with such sweet Divine Love, with such sweet, Divine Ecstasy. With such sweet, Divine Bliss that we shimmer and tingle and sparkle with the beautiful, Divine Love. Deep, healing breath.

Feel this now. Know this is who you truly are. And at this moment, see your life exactly as you would have it be by laughing in your mind's eye, by giggling, by feeling a distinct joy, by knowing marvelous things are happening. See yourself pumping your fist because you are so happy and so excited. See yourself bouncing up and down like a child. See your child energy coming in and staying to play with you awhile. See the Divine Light filling every cell of your mind, body, and spirit, remembering who you truly are.

Practice your Violet Flame daily. Practice your Violet Flame when things seem too hard. Practice your Violet Flame when people make you feel less than you truly are so that you may be the light; you may be the love; you may be the peace. And call on your Archangels any time you need them. They love you so much. They worship you more than you could ever, ever know. You are the Divine Light of the God/dess energy. You are a brilliant, Shining Star. You are a powerful, powerful, loved creator, and the whole, Universal, Divine Love Force, Archangel force, Violet Flame force, is here for you now. And now that you know, things will only get better and better. Remember, "I am the Violet Flame. I am the light of God/dess creation." Remember that. So mote it be. So it is. Great blessings to you and yours. Divine Love. Thank you, Archangels and Violet Flame.

4

ANGELIC MANIFESTATION JOURNAL BONUS

Create more of the life you want with the Archangels as you explore and focus with your Angelic Journal. If you are ready, let's set intentions now to make your Archangel Violet Flame Book a Manifestation tool. It is said that humans have so many thoughts going on in our heads at once that it is hard for Angels and Spirit Guides to hear what we want help with. This is one of the many reasons it is so powerful to get very clear on what we desire and write it out in a designated journal for our Archangels. This way, they can understand our needs better and help us with our dreams and goals in Divine Time.

It has been proven that when we write things down, more of what we desire comes to us. Goals get accomplished, and things flow with more ease. Adding the Amazing Archangels to your journaling just makes the results that much stronger. As we set intentions for what we want and take the time to focus and write it down in our journal, unseen forces move on our behalf. We are going to enlist the help of this Divine Knowing with our Archangel book in an interactive way and turn our book into a manifestation tool. We are also going to play with our books like children and have some fun. Children are powerful creators, and we will take on some of their great habits for their creative value.

Focus and underline ideas you resonate with in your book and become immersed in Upliftment. There is a deeper connection as we become interactive with our Archangel books. We may get colored pens and underline areas of our book that feel important or special to us. We may want to draw pictures of desired blessings or anything that makes us feel good. We may want to mark different areas of our book with hearts, stars, or Angel wings. Get sticky tab notes, a personal favorite, and stick them to your favorite pages you want to return to often. In your journal section, place a sticky tab on an area you want to let the Angels know to help you write in and as a personal reminder. Let your Angelic interaction and intuition guide you with what feels best. Neville Goddard and Albert Einstein both explained that our imagination is a creative force and can bring great blessings to our lives. We will bring our imagination fully into our process now. You may want to add stickers to enhance pages. Place a beautiful angel or magic looking card in your book as a bookmark. Get creative and give your book some personal character. Putting clover or flowers in your book to press and dry, adds some powerful nature magic to your process. Roses are a great choice as they have the highest vibration of any flower. You may give lovely flowers as an offering to your Archangels as well. Giving back is always a beneficial activity.

Everyone has magical abilities. Some of

us know this, and some do not. My point is all these ideas are simple and will work for anyone who puts forth an effort and has the faith to relax and let go so the angels may do their work. Of course, anything we put out comes back to us, so we want to always include "for the highest good" in all requests.

In all my studies of magical herbs, cinnamon is found in many different traditions for enhancement of all things wanted and removing things not wanted. You may want to rub a dab of cinnamon mixed with a touch of olive oil on your journal in an intentional shape such as a heart for more love or the infinity symbol for more abundance. Then say to yourself, "I anoint my journal with success and happiness with the help of the Archangels." Anointment has been practiced for eons with much luck and advancement. Basil and Sage could just as easily be utilized. Anything that feels magical and speaks to you in your spice cabinet most likely has wonderful magical properties. Use these gifts of nature with intention and focus for a more joyous life. The idea is to create a magnet for all you desire that is for your highest good with your Archangel Journal.

You may want to underline ideas in colors that mean something to you. The sky is the limit, get creative and juicy with your book, knowing that amazing things are being created.

Next, we have dedicated pages that are waiting for you to fill them with your heart's desires that the Violet Flame and Archangels will help you achieve as long as they are for the highest good. You may write anything you want in your Archangel Journal. There is no right or wrong way to do this. You may ask the Archangels to help you release things from your life, share your hopes and dreams, or ask questions. I ask my angels questions, patiently wait, and know they will lead me to the answer in Divine Time.

Be open and honest with your journaling and the Archangels understanding that the only ones who need to see your Angel Journal are you and your Angels. Keeping your wishes to yourself is very powerful for manifesting as well.

We have created categories for you, and

of course, there will Be freestyle areas, so play with this and have fun. After you play with your journal, you may put it away in a sacred space knowing all is in Divine Order. Remember, magic works just in its own time and asking where the results are will only block things, so relax, have faith, and patience. Keep this dream book; you will be pleasantly surprised when you check on it at later dates. You may come back to read your Violet Flame book and add more to it at any time. Know that unseen beneficial forces are moving to help you now and forevermore. Play with and collect other Archangelology books and audios, remembering, "If you call them, they will come." Check out the Archangelology Archangel Journaling Book for more ideas on taking your Journaling Process to the next "celestial" level. The Archangels have tied this whole series Together for us in such a Divinely Intelligent way. Spend time in nature with your book, filling it with love, imagination, and Angelic magic for exponential results. You are a powerful creator and loved by all that is.

Write on the blank areas of your book

and on the lined journal areas. Think outside of the box and let your kid like creative energies flow. Have fun, and add your own flair.

Please enjoy the process and expect wonderful things.

5

VIOLET FLAME JOURNALING

Write out all the places in your life you would like to infuse with the Violet Flame for more Love, Light, Abundance, Peace and more. Get creative and juice with new ways to utilize the Violet Flame to enhance your life for the highest good.

VIOLET FLAME ABUNDANCE

Write out how you would like Archangel Raphael and the Violet Flame to help you bring more Abundance and Well-Being to your life.

RELATIONSHIP JOURNALING

C reate some secret Love Letters with Archangel Haniel.

I FOCUS ON FEELING MY HIGHEST GOOD.

Spend some time with Archangel Metatron and the Violet Flame, creating more Vitality.

7

FINANCIAL BLESSINGS JOURNALING

M y financial goals are accomplished with the help of the Violet Flame.

**I AM ABUNDANTLY BLESSED
FOREVER FREE.**

8

PERSONAL JOY JOURNALING

I AM attracting things that bring me joy and bliss with the help of the Violet Flame.

I AM FINDING FUN THINGS TO DO.

THE FUN IS JUST BEGINNING.

Call on Archangel Gabriel to help you get your creative juices flowing for more fun.

FREESTYLE JOURNALING FOR A
BLESSED LIFE

Fill these pages with any fun and unique ideas that you desire your Archangels to help you line Up. Have fun. Get out your colored pens. Draw dolphins, fancy cars, Unicorns, and anything that makes you smile.

I AM LETTING MY CREATIVE
ENERGIES FLOW

10

JOURNALING FOR NEW PROJECTS

I deas for new projects the Violet Flame help me bring to Life for the highest good.

I AM THE VIOLET FLAME IN ACTION I AM THE VIOLET FLAME

P lay with your Violet Flame for more Self Love and Confidence.

11

JOURNALING YOUR GRATITUDE

F ill these pages with the things you are truly grateful for. Let the Archangels and Divine Energy know how much you appreciate them. Draw pictures for them as gifts or press clovers or flowers here as offerings for all they do for you.

I AM GRATEFUL FOR ALL THIS
AND MORE

I LOVE THESE PEOPLE FOR THESE REASONS.

You are a lover, and when you find things to love about others, it helps you align with a wonderful feeling. Enjoy.

12

MY FAVORITE THINGS

Take time, get by yourself, and write a list of things you love to do. Write out things you love to think about that bring you peace, bliss, and Joy.

13

BLESSINGS

May the Divine Creative Force that Moves and Creates the Universes Bless and Enhance Every Wish You Ever Conceived that is for the Highest Good of All Involved. May Joy, Peace, and Purpose Be Yours all the Days of your Lives. Through All Time Space and Dimensions. So Mote it Be, and So It Is. I hope this book helps you in wonderful ways and radiates out to a gorgeous future for you and yours.

Kim

REFERENCES

Diana Cooper. The Archangel Guide to Ascension: 55 Steps to Light. (Hay House Inc. 2015)

Elizabeth Clair Prophet. Violet Flame, To Heal Body, Mind & Soul. (Summit Publications, Inc, 1997)

Esther and Jerry Hicks. The Essential Law of Attraction Collection. (Hay House).

Matias Flury. Downloads From The Nine: Awaken As You Read. (Matias Flury 2014).

14

MORE OFFERINGS

Visit https://archangelology.com/home to discover more Archangels and Super Power Saints

Each of the following books has a matching audio filled with healing music.

Archangelology Michael * Protection

Archangelology Raphael * Abundance

Archangelology Camael * Courage

Archangelology Gabriel * Hope

Archangelology Metatron * Well Being

Archangelology Uriel * Peace

Archangelology Haniel * Love

Archangelology Raziel * Wisdom

Archangelology Zadkiel * Forgiveness

Archangelology Jophiel * Glow

Archangelology Violet Flame * Oneness

Archangelology Sun Angels * Power

Archangelology Moon Angels *
Magnetism

Archangelology Sandalphon *
Harmony

Archangelology Orion * Expansion

The items below come in book only

Archangelology * Archangel Journaling

Archangelology * Archangel
Breath-Tap Book

How Green Smoothies Saved My
Life Book

Activate Your Abundance Book and Audio
Program

The rest of the items below are available in Audio Format

Archangelology Barachiel * Heavenly Blessings

Archangelology * Breath-Tap Super Power Saints Volume 1 Audio

Archangelology * Breath-Tap Super Power Saints Volume 2 Audio

Regeneration Meditations * Switchword Series with Solfeggio Frequencies audio

Radiating Divine Love * Switchword Series with Solfeggio Frequencies audio

Love Charm * Switchword Series with Solfeggio Frequencies audio

Dragon Sun Grounding Meditations * Cosmic Consciousness Series audios

Sweet Moon Sleep Meditation * Cosmic Consciousness Series

Enchanted Earth Sacred Geometry * Cosmic Consciousness Series audios

15

SUPER POWER SAINTS BREATH-TAP AUDIOS

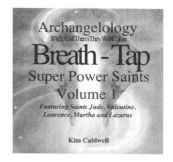

Learn more at https://archangelology. com/home

16

BE AN ANGEL

I f you enjoyed this book or received any help from it please give it a positive review so others may find it as well. Thank you so much for your time and help.

Kim

Printed in Great Britain
by Amazon